Toilet Material

Very Short Stories for
Very Short Attention Spans

ROBBIE PICKARD

All artwork and design by T. Jay Santa Ana.

Copyright © 2017 Robbie Pickard

All rights reserved.

ISBN: 1545140081
ISBN-13: 978-1545140086

To my wife, Alyse

AUTHOR'S NOTE

None of the stories you're about to read are real.
Except three of them. Guess which ones.

CONTENTS

Introduction: My First (And Second) Time	1

Part 1: Disaster

My First Gray Hair	9
The Abduction	12
Adult Toy Store	15
Sunglasses at Night	17
My First Day in Prison (If I Took My Friend Kevin's Advice)	19
The Seagull Snatcher	23
The Three Ways Doomsday Preppers Will Die	27
What It's Like to Have Herpes (According to Herpes Medication Commercials)	30
Vegas Isn't Ready	33

Watching True Crime TV Shows	36
If I Got Hired at Apple's Genius Bar	38
The Only Apology from the Guy Who Used This Gas Station Bathroom Before Me That Would Make Sense	42

Part 2: Love

My Wife's Dream Restaurant	47
Checking Out Girls	50
How Martian Babies Are Made	52
The Night They Signed Their Prenup	56
Rocket Science	59
How to Get Your Daughter's Boyfriend Out of the Picture for Good	62
Jeff Fingered Amy on Space Mountain	63
Love is Love	66
North Dakotan Phone Sex	69
The Birds and the Bees and Magic Johnson	72
Viagra and Earplugs	75
Troy's Dream Trip to Hawaii	77

Part 3: Honesty

Adult Beverages	85
Dear Owner of The Bra I Just Found Hanging in a Tree	88
A Play-by-Play Account of the 26 Hours and 11 Minutes My iPhone Was Being Fixed	90
The Eccentric Millionaire	93
Fortune Cookie Writer's Block	95
Millennial High School Reunions	98
Childhood Ambitions	100
Reviewing Online Reviewers	101
Last Meal	104
A Poet Who Doesn't Know It	107
A Minnesotan Sandwich	108
Group Chats ... in Real Life	112
Praying for Victory	115
A Eulogy to My Final Erection	118

Acknowledgments

About the Author

INTRODUCTION:
MY FIRST (AND SECOND) TIME

Ask any comedian to tell you their comedy birthday and they'll give you an exact date—the day they stepped on stage to perform stand-up for the first time.

My comedy birthday is May 11, 2007.

I'm not proud of chugging a tall can of Coors Light and listening to DMX's "Ruff Ryder's Anthem" on repeat by myself in the car that day, but that's exactly what happened. That cool, refreshing taste of the Rockies would slow my heart rate down a little, and then, *"Stop, drop, shut 'em down, open up shop"* followed by a couple of DMX barks would ramp it right back up. It was like a Red Bull and vodka—I was just breaking even.

It wasn't a great idea, but it was the best plan I could think of as I waited in the parking garage of The Ice House Comedy Club in Pasadena, California, 45 minutes before the start of the show.

My crippling anxiety was somewhat eased by

the fact that I had begged all of my friends to come see me perform and about 25 of them were in attendance, giving me guaranteed laughs from 20 percent of the crowd no matter how terrible I was up there.

As I was brought onstage and nervously rambled through my first few jokes, I felt my right leg beginning to shake. I had visualized failure up there in a hundred different ways, but involuntary leg spasms hadn't been one of them. Most of them involved completely forgetting my jokes the second I got onstage, and just standing there silently like an idiot while everyone booed. But now all I could think about was whether or not the crowd could tell that I was literally trembling in fear.

Just then, a waitress began to walk down the aisle in my direction. *Oh great, I'm about to get kicked off the stage for not being funny enough.*

Luckily that wasn't the case. My buddy Brian was in the crowd and, sensing my nerves, had bought me a shot of Jägermeister. The waitress was just bringing it up to the stage for me. A spontaneous chant of "Shot! Shot! Shot!" broke out from the crowd.

Two years before this I was living in a fraternity house. Being on stage in front of a group of people may have been very new to me, but chugging alcohol in front of a group of chanting drunks was not.

I gulped it down and the crowd went crazy.

The combination of the shot, the tall can of Coors Light, and having a packed house rooting me on had stopped my leg from shaking. Suddenly, I was fearless. Liquid courage at its finest.

The crowd laughed hysterically when I told them that I can't read Braille, but I bet the Braille at drive-thru ATM machines probably says, "How did you get here? Please have someone else drive home." They laughed even harder when I closed with the idea that I should make every important life decision immediately after sex, as it's the only time men are levelheaded. I ended with an act out of me having sex and then immediately nailing a job interview. The crowd ate it up.

I had "killed," as comedians say.

After the show, an important-looking man came up to me and said he ran a comedy show at a bar in West Covina, and would love to have me perform. He was in a suit and I was in baggy jeans, Vans sneakers, and an RVCA t-shirt. He was obviously a big deal in the industry. I was on top of the world.

After a long day of filing papers at my temp job the following Thursday, I drove to West Covina, ready to kill for a second time. But this was nothing like the show at The Ice House. This time none of my friends were there, and I had forgotten my lucky tall can of Coors Light. Most of the audience wasn't even aware there was going to be a stand-up comedy show until the man in the suit (the same suit) turned off all the TVs in the bar, right in the middle of the fourth quarter of the Colts-Steelers game, and grabbed a microphone. He told one joke about making love to a G-MILF, the mother of a mother he'd like to "F." It didn't go over very well, and then he brought me onstage as "Bobbie Pickford."

I did my same five minutes of material from the big show at The Ice House, word for word. I paused for laughter at the end of each well-rehearsed bit, but it never came. A man in a Steelers jersey stared me down the entire time. He didn't give a shit about my drive-thru ATM bit—he was too busy seething with anger that a Ben Roethlisberger game-winning drive was probably taking place and he was missing it. That room felt like the quietest place on Earth, which is pretty tough for a crowded bar full of pool tables.

I had "bombed," as comedians also say.

Over the thousand or so times I've gotten on stage since that day, I've killed, bombed, and everything in between. But my favorite thing about stand-up has always been the moment I came up with a new joke idea. There's something indescribably fulfilling about having a silly idea pop into your head, writing it on a napkin or texting it to yourself, then getting up in front of a group of strangers later that night and having them laugh along with you. It's human connection at its purest.

I wrote this book based on hundreds of those notes, texts, and voice memos. Now, instead of driving to a comedy club, buying a ticket, and adhering to a mandatory two-drink minimum, we can connect on all of these silly ideas from the comfort of your own toilet. It's like I'm right there in the bathroom with you!

Just sit down, flip to any page, knock out a couple of chapters and flush—which just so happens to be the same way I wrote it.

Part 1

Disaster

MY FIRST GRAY HAIR

There's got to be some kind of mistake, I thought. There's just no fucking way this is what I think it is.

I shifted hair back and forth, hoping it was a mirage. I tried to blame it on poor lighting or a weird glare.

But there was no glare. And the lighting was fine. I was officially the owner of a real-life gray hair.

What's next? Sweatpants? Velcro shoes? Early bird specials? A walker with tennis balls attached to the legs?

I bet Alzheimer's is next. Holy shit, it could already be here. No one actually says, "I have Alzheimer's." Other people tell them they have Alzheimer's and then they forget. How cruel is that? Sometimes my grandfather forgets that the TV remote isn't the telephone. He'll try to call me with the remote pressed against his ear and end up in a one-sided conversation with Lester Holt on

Dateline NBC. I'm not there yet, am I?

Nope, there's no denying this gray hair is very real. I have to do something about it. The way I see it, there are only three options:

PLUCK IT

That's the easy way out, right? I could simply pluck it and pretend it never existed. No one knows about this thing yet, and I've successfully buried secrets far worse than this one.

I dug around the bathroom drawer and pulled out a "manscaping kit" my then-girlfriend-now-wife had bought me years ago. I pulled out the tweezers and positioned them at the base of the problem.

Then I remembered reading that plucking a gray hair only ends up causing 10 more gray hairs to sprout up in that same spot. Seeing how one gray hair has made me borderline psychotic, I don't want to see what 10 would do.

HIDE IT

If I can't pluck it, maybe I can at least sweep it under the rug for now? I tried brushing hair to one side and then to the other. Both looked equally bad. Comb-overs are like those orange camouflage pants people used to wear—you really aren't hiding anything.

EMBRACE IT

I could simply man up and accept my new gray hair. After all, gray hair equals life experience, right? It makes a man look wise. Like he's been places and learned important things along the way. I trust a professor with gray hair over one with a full head of black hair. What does that guy know?

And hey, George Clooney has had gray hair for years—and he was voted Sexiest Man Alive! And Just For Men even has a salt-and-pepper dye kit! Maybe this is a blessing in disguise. Maybe this isn't so bad.

Besides, I bet every guy feels like this when he finds the first gray hair on his balls.

THE ABDUCTION

Amid a sea of lights and microphones, a very nervous Eric Davis stood at the podium as the press conference began.

"So many reporters. I wasn't expecting this leaving the hospital. Oh well, here goes.

"My name is Eric Davis, and it's true. Last week, I was abducted by extraterrestrial creatures and taken aboard their spacecraft for approximately 24 hours. I cannot guarantee that they didn't erase some of what I saw and heard before sending me back to Earth, but here's what I remember:

"As I lay sound asleep, a bright green light came in to my room. The door opened. There were no sounds, except for an ominous hiss of an engine coming from just outside my bedroom wall. A gray figure appeared out of the shadows. He did not speak, but held out one finger signaling, 'Come with me.'

"He spoke to me telepathically, and it was as if our thoughts were one. I'm here to tell you that these incredibly intelligent, kind, and courteous creatures come in peace. They are desperate to warn us of the perils we face due to the way we're treating our beautiful planet."

A reporter took Eric's brief pause as a sign to jump in.

"Hi, Roger Buckley here. Channel Six News. Did it hurt when they inserted the anal probe?"

"I beg your pardon?" asked Eric.

"The probe that the aliens use for research purposes," Buckley continued. "The one that was inserted anally. I think we're all just curious how badly it hurt."

"I think you've seen one too many movies," replied Eric. "Now, as I was saying, the gray figure spoke to me, but never moved his mouth. He was using telepathy. Another figure entered the room, and they both flooded my brain with information. I was completely awestruck.

"They told me they had serious concerns about the power plants littering our planet, and that they've moved toward wind and solar power with great results. They admitted that at one time, they too were destroying their planet. The only reason they came here was to pass their teachings along so that we may be able to save Earth, too."

"But did they offer any hints on how the anal

probes work?" shouted the Channel 11 reporter.

"I'm not even going to acknowledge that question. This isn't a joke, I was actually abducted and spent over 24 hours in a UFO," said Eric.

"They explicitly discussed the importance of reducing greenhouse gas emissions. I mean, these beings are 500 years ahead of us in every conceivable way! We should heed their warnings. I repeat: Their intentions are good. We should take them seriously because—"

"Hi, Roger again. Channel 6. Can't you give us something better than that? Al Gore said most of that stuff years ago.

"I think we're still all blown away that aliens can learn so much about humans through our asses. Would you not agree that's pretty crazy? Since the abduction, have you ever looked at your own in the mirror? Like, just to investigate?"

"Yeah," said the guy from Channel 11. "Did you see or feel them do anything that could help us learn more about ourselves through our own buttholes?"

"That's it! I think we're done here," said Eric, walking away from the podium with a noticeable limp.

ADULT TOY STORE

JERRY: Hello sir, do you happen to have the *Star Wars* edition of Monopoly?

STORE CLERK: Excuse me?

JERRY: The *Star Wars* edition of Monopoly. Do you have it in stock?

STORE CLERK: I think you're in the wrong place, buddy.

JERRY: I don't think so, buddy. The sign out front says, "Adult Toys." We're having a couple's game night at our place this Thursday, and everyone's leaving their kids behind with a babysitter. I'm in charge of the games.

STORE CLERK: Well, the only *Star Wars* thing I have is this blowup doll of Princess Leia.

JERRY: Hmm, that might work. But she's a little weird looking. Why is her mouth all wide open like that?

STORE CLERK: Let's just say she's surprised.

JERRY: Well, at $250 that makes two of us, but my wife will kill me if I screw this up again. I'll take it.

SUNGLASSES AT NIGHT

"Ugh, look at that douchebag," said Steve, in between sips of his whiskey and coke.

"Dude ... sunglasses at 11 p.m.?" Jason replied. "That's exactly what's wrong with this bar. It's turning into another goddamn hipster hangout."

"It's changing fast, that's for sure," Steve agreed. "A couple years ago, I'd walk into this bar and recognize nearly every single person. All locals. Now there's a ridiculously long line to get in, and I hardly see a familiar face."

Jason and Steve ordered another round.

"You can hardly call this a dive bar now. It's gentrification, man. Rich assholes trying to push their materialistic lifestyle on us. I'm telling you, if it wasn't for rent control, we'd get pushed outta here so fast," said Jason.

"Holy shit, Sunglasses Guy's friend might be even worse. He brought his fucking dog to the bar," Steve grumbled into his glass as he took another swig.

"That's even more hipster than the sunglasses! I bet they're bragging to the waitress about how it's a rescue," said Jason.

"People say I rescued him," said Steve, in his best wimpy dog owner impersonation. "But he's given me so much love and purpose ... I say little Boomer here is the one who rescued me."

Now three whiskey and cokes deep, Jason hit his limit.

"I'm gonna go say something to them."

"Dude, don't. Not worth it."

"No, man. Someone has to step up. This is *our* bar, and we can't just sit back and watch these tight-jeaned, sunglasses-at-night hipsters stomp all over the culture we've built here!"

Just as Jason was getting up, the two hipsters stood up to leave. Sunglasses Guy pulled out a white cane with a red tip and aimed it out in front of him to start walking. His friend picked up the dog's leash, making sure the yellow reflective strap marked "Service Dog" was secure across the dog's chest as they made their way toward the exit.

"Oh, shit," mumbled Jason, sitting back down in his seat.

"Whatever," said Steve. "This place is still changing."

MY FIRST DAY IN PRISON
(If I Took My Friend Kevin's Advice)

Aryan Anthony was assigned to show me around, and he's been really nice to me. I hardly notice the Swastika tattoo on his forehead anymore. We scanned the lawn during rec hour, and it didn't take long to spot the biggest, toughest prisoner around—Darnell "Stabby" Stapleton.

I quickly learned that Stabby isn't one of those ironic nicknames, like calling your 350-pound friend "Tiny." Stabby loved stabbing people, and he was quite good at it.

"He even stabbed himself in the side one time just to see how it felt," Aryan Anthony explained, as he finished carving a "KKK" tattoo on his calf.

Even from across the yard, the sight of Stabby raised the hair on my forearms. He genuinely scared the shit out of me. Just then I remembered the advice my friend Kevin gave me on his parent's couch a couple of years ago while we were watching an episode of *Locked Up Abroad*.

"It's not that big a deal," Kevin mumbled in between bong rips. "If you ever go to prison, just walk up to the biggest guy there—day one—and knock his ass out. Boom!

"I'm telling you, everyone's gonna respect you, and you'll live like a king. Oh, and cigarettes are like money in there. That's a big one."

I should probably tell you a little about Kevin.

He grew up in a sprawling mansion nestled in the hills of Palos Verdes Estates, one of the wealthiest neighborhoods in Southern California. He doesn't have a criminal record and likely never will. Even if he did something terrible, his father is a prominent defense lawyer and he'd never see the inside of a cell. But, he had recently Netflixed every episode of *Locked Up Abroad* and *Gangland,* so he had some serious knowledge to pass along.

I wasn't sure if I believed him, but now that I was in prison, his was the only plan I had. If I was going to survive in here, Stabby had to go down.

Lunch would be the best time to do it. There were a ton of guards in the cafeteria—a fight wouldn't last longer than a few seconds. If I got my sucker punch in quickly, the guards would be on top of Stabby and me before he could retaliate.

As the chef slumped an ice cream scooper full of mashed potatoes next to my rubbery slab of steak, I heard Stabby's boisterous voice from the back of the cafeteria. As you might expect, Stabby doesn't wait in line. He started pushing his way past all of us.

I had to strike right now. My heart was beating out of my chest, like I was standing at the edge of an airplane about to skydive for the first time.

"What do you think you're doing?" I shouted. Stabby turned around, and I slammed my lunch tray squarely across his face. Rubber steak and mashed potatoes flew across the room.

Stabby landed face first on the linoleum floor. Normally, his henchmen would've destroyed me in seconds, but they were in absolute shock. They had never actually had to back him up before. Sure enough, guards rushed to the scene and had both of us with our arms behind our backs. Stabby didn't even say anything; he just stared at me.

After what seemed like an eternity of silence, the prisoners all stood up and cheered. Someone had finally stood up to the biggest bully in the pen.

I spent the next two weeks in solitary confinement for my assault on Stabby, and I spent most of that time daydreaming of the hero treatment I'd get when I was released back to general population. I actually had a dream that a member of the Mexican Mafia slid half a pack of Parliaments under my door. I don't even smoke, but in my fantasy I tucked them under my mattress, as he gave me a silent nod of respect.

The day I got out of solitary, Stabby did too. I'll spare you the details, but boy did he get his revenge. I mean he really let me have it. Turns out he was not happy about the whole tray incident, and during those two weeks I was daydreaming about living like a king, Stabby had been daydreaming about what he was going to do to me.

He spared my life under the condition that I put a mop on my head, smear red Kool-Aid on my lips, and become his girlfriend.

For the rest of my sentence, no other inmates bothered me. Stabby protected me, because I was *his* bitch. So, I guess my friend Kevin's advice kind of worked.

THE SEAGULL SNATCHER

"Is one coming?" I shouted through the towel draped over my body.

"Yes! Shut the hell up!" Matt snapped. "You'll scare it away!"

Everything was going to plan. I lay quietly in the shallow, body-sized hole my friends and I had dug, with my arms stretched over my head. Matt, Ryan, and Taylor draped my blue Quicksilver beach towel over me, and sprinkled a few Flamin' Hot Cheetos on top for bait. After that, it was simply a waiting game. We were ready to catch ourselves a seagull.

I jumped at the chance to be the one under the towel, picturing myself holding up a seagull in triumph. As I sweated underneath the hot towel baking in the sun, I imagined strangers cheering and looking at me in awe in the not-too-distant future.

It wasn't long before the first seagull showed up.

Matt, Ryan, and Taylor created a circle around me 10 yards across so no one would scare off the lone, brave gull waddling toward me and our snare.

"Don't breathe so hard," said Ryan. "I can see the towel going up and down."

I held my breath. The tension was palpable. A small crowd had gathered to watch us in action. The seagull moved swiftly toward the six Flamin' Hot Cheetos left unattended and ripe for the picking.

After a slight pause to plan his transition from sand to towel, the seagull climbed on top of my stomach and grabbed a beak full of Cheetos in his moment of triumph.

"Now!" They all shouted.

I felt the adrenaline surge and sprang into action. In one fluid motion I took the top corners of the towel and snapped them down to my toes in what was essentially the world's fastest sit-up, clasping all four corners of the towel together like a trash bag. Success!

I held my towel full of seagull like a proud fisherman holding up a prize Bluefin. You could see a lump moving underneath the towel as the seagull frantically searched for an escape route.

I was smiling ear to ear. We were all smiling ear to ear.

Then, a pause.

A pause because no one knew what to do next. We hadn't come up with a game plan for when we actually caught one. This was uncharted territory.

"What do I do now?" I yelled, as the seagull continued to bounce around inside of my towel.

"Swing it around so it calms down," said Ryan.

"Let's take it home with us!" suggested Matt.

"Kill it!" yelled Taylor.

I knew I wasn't taking Taylor's suggestion, but I still didn't know what to do. The seagull was showing no signs of letting up on his Tasmanian Devil-like surge for freedom. Out of ideas and patience, I dropped the towel and the seagull took off in a hurry, making an awful squawking noise as he flew away. The crowd clapped and cheered. They were really into it. We should've charged admission. No one could believe we had actually caught a seagull.

I was a hero! It was just like I had pictured it while sweating my ass off under that towel. The Seagull Snatcher. That's what they'd probably call me from now on.

But as I bent down to pick up my towel, I noticed something.

The terrified seagull had shit half of his bodyweight all over my brand new, fluffy blue Quicksilver beach towel. The one my very first girlfriend had got me for my birthday.

"Oh, dude. That is so fucking gross!" said Taylor.

A trail of white paste lay strewn across my forearm, and it wasn't sunscreen. I walked toward the ocean to rinse off.

"Babe, you should've seen that seagull shit all over that guy's towel!" a beachgoer said as he pointed me out to his girlfriend.

THE THREE WAYS DOOMSDAY PREPPERS WILL DIE

People who believe the end of the world will come during their lifetime spend most of their time on YouTube learning how to build a self-sustaining aquaponics system to feed their families. Seems like a waste when there are only three ways a Doomsday Prepper will die:

1. Nothing happens, and you die (eventually).

Okay, you spent your whole life preparing for something that never happened. So what? You have more canned goods than anyone in your zip code! And if something would've happened, everyone totally knows you would've been the last one standing.

Who cares if you spent your entire life savings building a "bug-out" vehicle instead of taking vacations with your family or sending your kids to college? They got a *real* education when you took them into the woods every weekend to teach them how to set booby traps for when the zombie neighbors invade! They can pass on that knowledge to their children. See, it wasn't a waste!

Your kids will still thrive, even in a world that doesn't fall apart. You've taught them fantastic social skills, so long as they're in an underground bunker and the topic of conversation is about how honey is the only food that will never spoil. I see future beekeepers!

2. Something happens, but you die anyway.

Ugh, what a bummer! Your $250,000 underground compound was ready and raring to go, and a nuclear bomb was detonated and caused an apocalyptic electromagnetic pulse just like you said it would. The problem is, you didn't get to say "I told you so" because you weren't near your bunker when this happened and died along with all of the idiotic unprepared. That's just shit luck, man! You're in that bunker 22 hours of the day, what are the odds? Hey world, I'd like a do-over, please!

3. Something happens and you survive!
(Until you die.)

Ding! Ding! Ding! You hit the lotto! Your dream scenario played out, and the world as we know it has been destroyed. That moat around your house is put to good use, as the unprepared survivors pathetically attempt to gain access to your compound. As the bodies of unsuccessful invaders drift across the scummy water, and you and your family get to laugh and sip on purified rainwater.

Those who foolishly tried to enjoy their lives before the apocalypse slowly die off, while you and your family feast on the bounty of dehydrated food you put in the cellar years ago.

Slowly, however, you realize that you now live in a world where the entire population consists of people who were Doomsday Preppers. Those are the only people you have to hang out with. Forever. You beg for a second apocalypse.

WHAT IT'S LIKE TO HAVE HERPES
(According to Herpes Medication Commercials)

DOCTOR: Sorry to keep you waiting. I have your results.

MICHELLE: Well? What is it?

DOCTOR: I'm afraid it's positive. You have herpes.

MICHELLE: Oh my God. So, what do I do now?

DOCTOR: I know this isn't pleasant news, but I assure you that there are millions of people living with genital herpes. And while we can't guarantee complete remission, we can dramatically reduce outbreaks and you will lead a normal life—with a few minor restrictions.

MICHELLE: Okay … what are my options?

DOCTOR: There are a few ways we could go. What are you currently doing for recreation?

MICHELLE: I beg your pardon?

DOCTOR: Recreation. Do you run? Play any sports?

MICHELLE: My job keeps me pretty busy. I try to get to the office gym once or twice a week. Mostly the elliptical machine.

DOCTOR: So you don't own a kayak, mountain bike, or pair of skis?

MICHELLE: No! I live in Omaha.

DOCTOR: All right, I'm going to write a prescription for all three. You can pick them up at REI. Tell them I sent you.

MICHELLE: I don't want a kayak or a bike. Or skis. Isn't there a topical cream I should start using?

DOCTOR: *[stops writing, takes off glasses].* Let me be very clear here, Michelle. You have genital herpes. Things are going to be very different now. Outdoor activities must become your entire life.

MICHELLE: Huh? How does that help my herpes?

DOCTOR: It doesn't. There is no cure, but for reasons we don't fully understand, people with genital herpes are their happiest when they're biking or kayaking with other people who have genital herpes. Shared experiences, I suppose. Picture an outdoor club, like on MeetUp.com or whatever, but they can only join if they have herpes.

MICHELLE: I'm not sure I'm healthy enough to mountain bike. I have a bad knee.

DOCTOR: I suggest starting slow. Maybe do yoga by a lake somewhere. And it won't hurt you to smile while doing it.

MICHELLE: There aren't any lakes around me!

DOCTOR: I'm going to write you another prescription. This one is to move to Denver.

MICHELLE: What about my job?

DOCTOR: Health comes first.

MICHELLE: How will I make friends in Denver? I don't want to do all of these outdoor activities by myself.

DOCTOR: Go to any mountain, lake, or river and look for people on paddleboats, kayaks, or just stretching and laughing together. You won't even have to ask them, they'll just look right at you and say, "I have genital herpes."

MICHELLE: It's that easy?

DOCTOR: It's that easy. You'll do great.

VEGAS ISN'T READY

On May 4, 2016, Tracy took a photo with her two friends, all wearing cocktail dresses and ready to hit the club. She posted the picture on Instagram with the caption:

Vegas Isn't Ready ;)

The following is a 100-percent true account of just how ill-prepared Las Vegas was for Tracy, Alexis, and Tiffany that night ...

The girls blasted a Beyoncé playlist Tiffany had put together just for this trip, dancing like crazy around their cheap hotel room.

They poured shots of Smirnoff, did their makeup, and picked out their final outfits for the evening.

It seemed like just another night in Sin City until Tracy took a selfie and posted the now infamous picture and caption: Vegas isn't ready ;)

As they made their way down the MGM Grand elevator and onto the Strip, all hell broke loose. They were right. Vegas simply wasn't ready for them.

"Oh my God, look at those girls!" said one man in a shiny new suit, driving a Range Rover full of men arriving for a bachelor party. "How are those three women so damn confident?" Unable to take his eyes off the girls, he lost control of the car and caused a 14-car pile-up. Everyone in the Range Rover died instantly.

With all of the prostitutes walking up and down the Strip, grown men blowing their kids' college fund at the craps table, and other debauchery going on 24/7, you'd think that Las Vegas would be able to handle Tracy, Alexis, and Tiffany in their black, coral, and periwinkle spandex dresses. But you'd be dead wrong. Tracy's Instagram caption was no exaggeration.

"Shut it down!" screamed a bouncer. "Shut it all down!"

"These ladies are going to tear this city to the ground by sunrise!" a bystander told a reporter covering the 14-car pile-up. "Someone call the mayor!"

One man sipping a three-foot margarita had a particularly tough time.

"There's just something about those three girls! They look just like everyone else on the Strip, they're wearing what literally every girl at a nightclub wears, but there's just *something* different! I can't handle this!" he yelled, before hurling himself over the eighth story balcony to his death.

Tiffany assessed the mayhem around her.

"Wow, we totally run this city," she said to Alexis and Tracy.

"OMG," said Alexis. "You *have* to use that as the caption in your next Instagram post."

WATCHING TRUE CRIME TV SHOWS

REPORTER ON TV: Katie was a beautiful, intelligent 19-year-old girl with dreams to open her own veterinary hospital in her hometown of San Clemente, California. But that dream would never come to be. Her life was tragically cut short when an assailant broke into her apartment and murdered her in cold blood.

DAD: Ugh, we've seen this one!

SISTER: Yeah, definitely seen it. Her mom starts ugly-crying here pretty soon. Anything else on?

REPORTER ON TV: Katie was found stabbed to death with—

BROTHER: … a knife from her own kitchen. We know. Ugh.

[On TV: Katie's family is sobbing uncontrollably.]

MOM: It's always with a knife from her own kitchen. It's the same thing over and over. Hide your knives, folks!

SISTER: Change it, please. I'm *so* bored.

[Mom changes the channel.]

NEW REPORTER ON TV: A triple homicide in a town that hadn't seen a murder in 15 years...

DAD: Finally, a *new* murder! Pass me a beer, would you?

IF I GOT HIRED AT APPLE'S GENIUS BAR

ME: Hello, sir. Welcome to the Genius Bar. Did you have an appointment?

CUSTOMER: Yes, with Robbie at 1:45.

ME: That's me! How can I help you?

CUSTOMER: My MacBook is incredibly slow. I think it's broken.

ME: Let me take a look here.

CUSTOMER: It keeps doing that pinwheel thing. Look what happens when I try to open up Safari.

[Customer gently taps a few keys, trying to open up his browser.]

ME: Ah yes, there it is. The dreaded pinwheel.

CUSTOMER: It drives me absolutely insane.

ME: Have you tried shaking the mouse around?

CUSTOMER: I'm sorry?

[I shake the mouse around and slam it down on the desk.]

ME: You've gotta shake it around pretty hard. If that doesn't work, trying slamming it on the desk over and over.

CUSTOMER: Umm ...

ME: *[still shaking the mouse violently]* This hardly ever works, but I always start with it. Now for step two. Let's start pressing keys on the keyboard.

CUSTOMER: Oh, like a restart command. Which keys do you use for that?

ME: Doesn't matter. All of them, really. Just keep pressing. If it doesn't work, press harder!

[I slam down on the keyboard repeatedly, using all ten fingers.]

CUSTOMER: Hey, take it easy! You're going to break my keyboard.

ME: Ah, I think I know what the problem is.

CUSTOMER: Finally. What is it?

ME: We have to yell at it. You know, like, scare the computer into working.

CUSTOMER: Are you serious?

ME: Give me a little credit here, I'm a freaking Apple Genius. *[To the computer]* C'mon, you piece of shit! Go! Why won't you go?!

CUSTOMER: Can you please get someone else to help me?

ME: I got this, trust me. Let's try slamming the laptop open and closed a few times. And don't forget to keep yelling at it. Let's yell together.

CUSTOMER: I'm not going to yell at it.

ME: Are you kidding me? You've been pinwheeling for *five* fucking minutes! Just open up Safari, you piece of shit!

CUSTOMER: C'mon man. You're making a scene.

ME: Fuck you!

[Manager enters.]

MANAGER: Did you just curse at a customer?

ME: No, not at all. I was trying to get this nice young man's computer to work by yelling at it and slamming it on the desk over and over.

CUSTOMER: Are you hearing what this guy is saying? He's been doing this for the past five minutes. How did you hire this guy?

MANAGER: I'm so sorry, sir. You're completely right. Robbie, scoot over.

CUSTOMER: Thank you. Finally.

MANAGER: Robbie, I've told you this a thousand times. You can't press those keys so damn softly. If you want that pinwheel to go away, you gotta slam that fuckin' keyboard like a man!

[Manager slams down on the keyboard with both hands. The "J" pops off.]

CUSTOMER: You idiots just broke my keyboard! I'm not paying for this.

ME: Look, the pinwheel went away!

MANAGER: It sure did. Another success!

ME: *[to customer]* I guess that's why he's the manager, eh?

THE ONLY APOLOGY FROM THE GUY WHO USED THIS GAS STATION TOILET BEFORE ME THAT WOULD MAKE SENSE

Hey man, I feel awful about the condition of the men's room. It's all my fault, but please allow me to explain:

You see, I'm a total germophobe, so there's just no way I'm going to touch that handle to flush. I mean, do you ever stop to think about how many dirty trucker hands have been on that handle over the years? As they say, if it's yellow let it mellow.

Second, my bad about the pubes on the toilet seat rim. You probably walked into the bathroom and thought, "Who the hell sheds down there?" But it wasn't shedding. See, I noticed that I had one hair longer than the rest, and due to my severe obsessive-compulsive disorder (OCD), I had to pluck it. But then I noticed another. And another. So, you get it. I also had to make sure I had an even number of hairs left, which threw me off at a couple of different points in the plucking process. Bad news for you, but having all my pubic hairs the exact same length is pretty good news for me and my OCD, because now nothing bad will happen to me or my family.

I'm also really sorry that you had to catch me on the week of my gang initiation. I carved my gang's initials into the toilet seat (with gloves on, of course), which doesn't sound that badass, I know. But you should see the faces of our rival gang when they sit on the toilet, get up, and have *our* initials on their asses. I can't confirm that this actually happens, but I can't help but keep trying!

Lastly, sorry about the smell. That one is pretty straightforward. I mean, two chili dogs for two bucks dude!

Part 2

Love

MY WIFE'S DREAM RESTAURANT

My wife has a million questions about the menu, but our waiter never loses steam. Chaz's unwavering patience is just one of the things that makes this place my wife's dream restaurant.

Finally, she narrows her selection down to three options. She turns to Chaz.

"I can't decide if I want the chopped salad, the lemon chicken, or to splurge and go for the turkey burger …"

Then, she panics. "Oh, and the linguini with clam sauce looks good, too!"

Most waiters would just pick one of those for her and move on. Chaz isn't most waiters.

"We can place a few bites of each of those on one big plate for you if you'd like," he says, already jotting it down.

My wife's face lights up.

"Yes, please!" she replies.

"Anything else for you, miss?" Chaz asks, making sure not to call her "ma'am" and make her feel old.

"Well, I noticed the woman at that table ordered fries and they really look good. But a whole order of french fries is crazy. I mean, I just ordered *12 bites* of food."

Chaz doesn't skip a beat. "Here," he explains. "You can order your fries … individually."

She's like a puppy when its owner walks in the door after being away all afternoon.

"Oohh! I'll have three fries then. No, wait … five!" She turns to me. "Why not, right? It's date night."

"Go for it," I reply.

With her order as complete as it will ever be, I order a skirt steak for myself. Chaz sets off to share our order with the cooks who will now have to assemble 12 bites of four separate entrees and exactly five french fries. Oh, and "a little bit of garlic mayo, but not too much!"

Soon, our food arrives. It's delicious. The steak is tender and juicy, and I finish it all—not before letting my wife try it too, of course. As is customary in my wife's dream restaurant, bites from items she didn't order herself don't count toward her total number of calories for her meal.

Her plate is a work of art. All three bites of her chopped salad have a perfect balance of bacon and avocado. The lemon chicken and turkey burger have been put into bite-sized pieces for sampling, and smack dab in the middle of her plate sit three sets of tightly rolled linguini, each with just the right amount of clam sauce resting neatly on top. To the side sit exactly five french fries, with just enough garlic mayo to get the job done.

As Chaz clears our plates, he asks if we've left any room for dessert. I can tell my wife is interested, and she reminds me that she's really only had a few bites of food for dinner when you think about it.

She tells Chaz, "Well, I did have my eye on the lava cake."

"That's my personal favorite," he replies. "Our lava cake comes in three sizes—you can order a sliver, a bite, or you can lick the spoon our chef used to mix the batter."

"Oohh, I'll lick the spoon!" she says, elated.

"Excellent choice," Chaz replies.

He comes back with a spoon covered in gooey chocolate batter. My wife goes at it like an ice cream cone.

"I'm so glad we didn't order an entire piece of cake. That would've been way too much," she says, wiping chocolate batter off of her chin with her wrist.

CHECKING OUT GIRLS

Renaissance Era

REGINALD: Look at that woman over there. She's gorgeous.

ELRIC: Definitely. She's huge!

REGINALD: So huge. And pale, too! She must come from a wealthy family to be able to eat so much and never work in the fields and get tan like a peasant.

ELRIC: And she looks plenty big enough for child bearing, too!

REGINALD: I'd actually prefer her to be a little bigger, but she's the fattest one in this room so she'll have to do. I'm gonna go talk to her.

Now

ROB: Look at that woman over there. She's gorgeous.

EVAN: Definitely. So thin!

ROB: I can see her ribs right through her shirt. And so tan! She must come from a wealthy family to afford so many juice cleanses and spray tan sessions.

EVAN: And she's got that sexy thigh gap! Her legs are like the size of my wrists. So hot.

ROB: I'd actually prefer legs a little skinnier, but she's the most emaciated one in this room so she'll have to do. I'm gonna go talk to her.

EVAN: Oops, she fainted. Missed your chance!

HOW MARTIAN BABIES ARE MADE

BLADMORF: Hello, and welcome to Mars. We are very excited to have you here. Contrary to how we are depicted in films made by Earthlings, we Martians are a pleasant and welcoming species.

TIM: Thank you, Bladmorf. We're excited to be here. While this is technically for work, I'd be lying if Dennis and I didn't say we jumped at the chance to explore your lovely planet now that Earth's technology finally makes it possible.

BLADMORF: Not to mention write it all off as a business trip, eh?

TIM: Ha, that too!

BLADMORF: Now, what exactly does your company do back on Earth?

TIM: Dennis and I are advisors to Earth's health industry. Now that Earthlings and Martians are allies, we're looking for insight on how you operate in these areas, and how it might influence the way we move forward on Earth.

BLADMORF: Great! Anything in particular?

TIM: As you know, Earth can get pretty divisive about procreation from a political standpoint. Our main focus is coming up with solutions to help ease complications of the conception and birthing processes. To reduce, or hopefully eliminate complications that can affect both mother and child.

BLADMORF: Well you've come to the right place. You're standing in the lobby of one of 47 Martian procreation buildings.

TIM: Oh, I thought this was just a hospital. You have that many facilities dedicated to procreation?

BLADMORF: Yes, of course. This is where married, committed partners come to fill out their applications for baby Martians.

TIM: Excuse our ignorance here, but applications?

BLADMORF: We take the act of bringing a new Martian into the world very seriously. When a couple decides they would like to procreate, they must come into one of these offices every month for an entire Martian year. We question them on their parenting approaches, their commitment to one another, what their goals are, and then determine if they should be granted permission to create a baby Martian.

TIM: They have to receive permission?

BLADMORF: Of course. We have to be sure that the parents are committed to raising a successful, kind, driven new Martian who isn't going to be a total waste of space. I thought Earth was obsessed with tests, licenses and things like that. You need to pass a test to drive a car, right? Do couples not need to pass any tests in order to create a new Earthling?

TIM: No, it doesn't work like that at all. On Earth, a man and a woman conceive a child by having sexual intercourse.

[Bladmorf spits his Martian coffee across the room.]

BLADMORF: That's all it takes to make new Earthlings?!

TIM: Yes. The man's sperm is released inside of the woman's vagina, which then meets with her egg, and an Earthling forms about nine months later.

[Bladmorf, having just taken a new sip of coffee, now spits this sip across the room.]

BLADMORF: Zazaza! Excuse my laughter, but sex is such a carnal, impulsive act. I mean, you're so hopped up on hormones, you're basically high! You make the choice to create a new Earthling whenever you're horny?

TIM: Yes, well it's not like it happens every time. And I guess it's not completely a choice for us, it's more like there's a chance it will happen if you have sex.

BLADMORF: But still, we Martians discourage any decision-making while horny. Our mind-sets aren't fit to fly a space car in that state, let alone create a baby Martian. At the risk of sounding rude, I'm flabbergasted that a culture as sophisticated as your own has such a primitive procreation process. I mean hell, most times Martians are horny they end up rubbing their own zaltifs until they splorg!

TIM: Yeah, well Earthlings tend to do that too.

BLADMORF: Zazaza! What other big decisions do you make with erect zaltifs? Buy a house? Make financial investments? Zazazaza! Hey Glargamel, come over here. You gotta hear how Earthlings make babies ... it's absolutely insane!

THE NIGHT THEY SIGNED THEIR PRENUP

Alex: Well, glad that's over with. Those things are so dumb, right?

Sharon: Yep.

Alex: They're so pointless, you know? I mean, there's no chance that any of those policies will ever need to see the light of day. I love you, we're so on the same page, babe. I guess it's just like life insurance, or something. Even more rare, like tornado insurance! And they're aren't even any tornadoes around here! It's all so silly.

Sharon: Uh-huh.

Alex: My dad and mom got one, too. And they're still happily married 35 years later! I feel like there's this stereotype that if you get a prenup, people think you're assuming you'll get a you-know-what down the road … and that's not the case at all! It's more like, a fire extinguisher. See, 99.9% of the time a fire extinguisher is never used and just gathers dust. It's just prudent to have it, that's all.

SHARON: Yeah ... a fire extinguisher.

ALEX: I wish they just called it some type of insurance instead, you know? *Prenuptial agreement.* Ugh, that name! That's the problem! It would sound so much nicer and not have this stupid stigma attached.

SHARON: Yep.

ALEX: Anyway, I'm just glad that's behind us. I mean it's Friday after all. Date night. You know, the kids are at that sleepover tonight ...

SHARON: You know, as hot and bothered as I am after spending all afternoon splitting up all of our assets, I think going home sounds a lot better.

ALEX: Oh, c'mon, let's move past this. How about that steakhouse we've been meaning to go to?

SHARON: Okay, fine.

ALEX: Now we're talking!

SHARON: Cooking does sound pretty awful.

ALEX: Great! I'm definitely going to try their porterhouse. It's supposed to be huge.

SHARON: Don't worry, I won't try and take half.

ALEX: Sharon! It's not like that!

SHARON: You're right, it's not like it's your fucking jet ski.

ROCKET SCIENCE

Phillip wasn't used to someone else making the first move, but he liked it.

"I must make a mean martini," he joked.

"Shhh," Sophia responded, placing her index finger on his lips before kissing him again.

It wasn't long before she removed his shirt, then hers.

"Nice bra, but it's got to go," he quipped.

He decided on a one-handed bra removal he had seen on YouTube; so confident that he even went for it with his left hand. After fumbling around for what felt like hours, he brought in his right hand for reinforcement. It didn't help.

Sophia gently grabbed his hands to help him out. "Oh Phillip, it's not rocket science," she said with a smirk.

"You don't think I know that?" said Phillip. "I'm an aeronautical engineer at the Jet Propulsion Laboratory." And he would've told her that at the bar earlier if he wasn't already trying to overcome his nerdy appearance.

"Oh, I'm just teasing," she said, calmly. "It's a saying."

"I'm familiar with the saying," he said sternly. "And in fact, if taking off your bra *was* rocket science, it would be very similar to performing a Hohmann transfer." He couldn't resist showing off a bit.

She looked confused.

"It's when you're moving a spacecraft from one orbit to another—the same way I'm trying to move this bra from your boobs to the floor. It goes a little something like this."

Phillip began fumbling with her bra strap on her right shoulder as he continued his comparison.

"We're essentially using two engine impulses, one to move a spacecraft onto the transfer orbit and a second to move off of it."

He started to fumble with the other strap on her left shoulder with his left hand.

"We'd continue executing a nominal trajectory correction maneuver at orbit periapsis, thereby optimizing our delta-v usage," he continued.

"Very impressive. But can I just show you something quickly?" Sophia said, lifting her arms up to help him out. He gently pushed them back down.

"Don't worry, I got this," he assured her. "The

problem is that our main engine gimbals are not articulating for God knows what reason this time."

"Gimbals?" asked Sophia.

Phillip continued fumbling with her bra strap. "I don't care what anyone says. A Hohmann transfer is the right way to move a spacecraft from one orbit to another *and* to get this damn bra off your tits!"

Phillip began to yank at the back of her bra with both hands.

"Please let me help. I could've been topless like 10 minutes ago."

He smacked himself in the forehead. "But I'm a god damn rocket scientist! I can literally put satellites into space. How the fuck can I not get this thing off?"

"Will you just let me finish?" she insisted. "I was going to say, it's not rocket science ... it's just a front-hook bra."

HOW TO GET YOUR DAUGHTER'S BOYFRIEND OUT OF THE PICTURE FOR GOOD

DAUGHTER: Daddy, I'd like you to meet my boyfriend, Avery.

DAD: Avery? Ha, how funny. That's my wife's nickname for my penis. Long story. Anyway, nice to meet you ... Avery. You two have fun at the movies tonight.

JEFF FINGERED AMY ON SPACE MOUNTAIN

I probably had a lot of fun at my eighth-grade class trip to Disneyland. I bet we ran around Tom Sawyer Island for hours. I bet we rode the Matterhorn five or six times. I bet I got funnel cake caught in my braces. I bet we yelled *PENIS!* as loud as we could right when it got pitch black inside the Haunted Mansion, giggling to ourselves and ruining the experience for everyone else.

I bet a lot of things happened that day, but after all these years I only remember one thing: Jeff fingered Amy on Space Mountain.

That's the rumor that swirled around The Happiest Place on Earth that day, and it stuck with me far longer than that. I had yet to even kiss a girl on the mouth and here was Jeff—my same age, in my grade, getting to third base with a girl.

I looked at Jeff the way Spaniards probably looked at Christopher Columbus upon his return.

He was a brave explorer who had been to places the rest of us could only imagine. He was my idol.

I went to Disneyland with my wife recently, and told her about Jeff and Amy as we stood in the line for Space Mountain. We had a good laugh.

As we approached the front of the line, we were thinking the same thing:

"Jeff is a liar," she said, confidently.

"I know, right?" I replied. "Pitch black, twisting and turning at 65 miles an hour?"

She agreed. "If he didn't lie, poor Amy wasn't having any fun. I mean, ouch. You know?"

Back then, it had honestly never crossed my mind that the guy I was in awe of in eighth grade might've simply just lied to impress his friends. I mean think about it. We all lied to impress our friends back then. I had definitely been guilty of that. I told my friends I had surfed waves twice as high as they really were, that I pulled off skateboard tricks I definitely hadn't, and a bunch of other crap to make me sound cooler than I really was.

I remember my friend Kyle telling me that the best way to make out with a girl was to move your tongue in counterclockwise circles over and over, and that he had gotten a lot of compliments from girls for that move.

"Oh yeah. That's my move, too. Works every time," I said, even though I had never been to first base. We were both completely full of shit, but neither of us would ever admit it.

As we buckled our seatbelts and the cart started moving, I thought about how happy I was that my eighth-grade level of insecurity had dissipated over the years. Look at me now—a full-grown adult, riding Space Mountain with my wife.

"Hey, wanna yell *PENIS!* as loud as we can when it's all pitch black in here?" my wife asked. "It'll be funny."

"Yes I do," I replied.

LOVE IS LOVE

Dillin and Michael were the cutest couple you could imagine. They threw the best parties, and everyone knew it.

"Special delivery!" Ben said jokingly, as he and Blanche knocked on the open front door.

"Well if it isn't the newlyweds!" said Dillin, still touching up his hair and tucking in his shirt. He gave Blanche a big hug and a peck on the nose.

Michael, wearing a "Kiss the Chef" robe, wiped his hands clean and jogged over to meet them.

"I hope I'm not crossing a line here, but you two are going to have *the* most beautiful children."

"No line crossed, we're looking to have kids pretty quickly," said Ben. He and Blanche gave each other a half-crooked smile.

"I've always said that mixed couples have the most gorgeous offspring. I mean, have you *met* Charlene? She's half Chinese, half West Highland Terrier."

Charlene must've taken all the best attributes

from each of her parents, because she was flawless. Ben tried his best not to stare. She was tall, probably close to five foot eight, with a busty figure and legs for days. Her big brown eyes glistened in the light, her mouth open as she panted.

Blanche yelped with excitement. What are the odds? She was a Westie herself and couldn't help but give Charlene's bottom a little sniff.

Ben poured vodka and soda into a doggie bowl for Blanche and grabbed a beer for himself. Blanche and Charlene circled each other—sniffing, then barking, still feeling each other out a bit.

"I'm just so happy that the marriage laws opened up last year," said Ben. "Remember when everyone was like, 'What's next? A man and a dog?' Thank God they thought of it!"

"Hey, love is love," said Michael. "Just think about how great this is. You, a thirty-eight-year-old man, and Blanche, a five-year-old West Highland Terrier."

"Thirty-five in dog years," Ben reminded him.

"Of course," said Michael. "We are living in a time like no other."

"Hey, Janice and Whiskers are here!" Dillin exclaimed.

Sure enough, a gorgeous blond woman made her way through the front door, a confident looking male cat by her side.

"Just back from our honeymoon and ready to keep the party going!" said Janice, holding a bottle of Sauvignon Blanc.

Whiskers grazed his tail against Ben's leg as he walked past. Blanche snarled at him.

"Who does this guy think he is?" Ben asked.

"What's the deal with you and Whiskers?" asked Michael. "You've always had a thing with him."

"Marrying a dog makes sense!" Ben snapped. "Dogs are loving and loyal. But cats? Who the hell likes cats? Let alone falls in love with one."

"Please," Michael replied. "They're our dear friends, and they love each other. Love is love, right?"

"It's a fucking cat, man! They're one of the only animal species that kills for pleasure. Did you know that? You can feed them all the Fancy Feast they can stomach, and they'd still go out and torture a lizard to death. Just for fun."

Ben turned to Janice.

"Hey Janice, Whiskers doesn't love you. You know that, right? He only sticks around because you feed him and clean up his shit from the litter box."

"Screw you, Ben," Janice snapped. "You don't know him like I do!"

Just as she finished telling him off, Whiskers entered the room and plopped a dead mouse at her feet.

"Aw, he gave you a present," said Ben. "You're a lucky woman, Janice."

NORTH DAKOTAN PHONE SEX

GARY: I'm taking my shirt off.

LISA: Gary! You're terrible.

GARY: C'mon, now you take something off.

LISA: Well, alright. Jeez. I'll take my scarf off.

GARY: Scarf? We can do better than that.

LISA: I just walked in the door, Gary! I'm in the mudroom takin' my darn boots off. I'm not in California like you, am I?

GARY: I'm unbuckling my belt …

LISA: Okay, take it easy, mister! I'm taking my jacket off now.

GARY: Now we're talking! My belt and shirt are both off now. Your turn.

LISA: I'm gonna take my sweater off now. The one

Grandma Ruth gave me last Christmas.

GARY: Umm, okay. My shoes are off, just my pants left to go.

LISA: You're all worked up over there, aren't ya? Okay, I'm taking my pants off then.

GARY: Wow, you're ahead of me now.

LISA: Not so fast, Gar. I've got my long underwear under them.

GARY: Oh God.

LISA: You want this to be real, don'tcha?

GARY: Yes, okay. Well my pants are off now—I'm all yours.

LISA: Okay, okay. I'm just a couple of layers behind ya. Taking off my socks now.

GARY: Nice.

LISA: The wools one, first. Then I'll get the other pair.

GARY: Oh boy …

LISA: Don't you get impatient with me. You're the one that wanted this.

GARY: Okay. Is that long underwear off yet?

LISA: It sure is.

GARY: Perfect. Now what are you doing?

LISA: That was my long underwear bottoms. I'll go ahead and take the long underwear top off now, naughty boy.

GARY: That's hot. Now we're getting somewhere.

LISA: Okay, off come the mittens ...

GARY: You still had mittens on?

LISA: Two pairs. It's colder than heck outside. You wouldn't want me touching you with icicles for hands.

GARY: I guess that's true.

LISA: You know, I should've taken these darn things off first now that I think about it. I had such a hard time with the darn coat zipper.

GARY: You know what? Lie to me. I take it back, just lie to me. Please just tell me you're already naked.

Lisa: I want this to be real, Gary! Hang on. I'm taking off my mitten liners now ...

THE BIRDS AND THE BEES AND MAGIC JOHNSON

I was furious when I first learned that Magic Johnson was HIV positive. I was completely consumed by it.

I was also six years old.

After hearing about it on the news, I paced around the house for hours, shaking my head in disbelief. "I just don't get it," I kept muttering to myself as my parents looked on.

The phrase "HIV positive" made no sense to me. Positive meant good as far as I knew. I didn't get why everyone was so sad. *We should all be a little more HIV positive, guys!*

I also wasn't much of a basketball fan, or a Magic Johnson fan for that matter. Soccer and baseball were my sports, so this anger and frustration really came out of nowhere. But a news anchor in a fancy suit said that Magic Johnson being diagnosed as HIV positive was tragic, and he was on television—so that was enough to put me on a real downward spiral. *I just don't get how this could have happened!*

Finally, my dad had enough of my pacing and decided to dive in. He was a little sick of the Magic Johnson pity party when it was brought on through him sleeping around.

"Do you really want to know this happened?" he asked.

I shook my head yes.

"Okay. Do you know about sex?" he continued.

"Yeah, do you?"

"I guarantee I know more about it than you do," he replied.

I shrugged.

"So you know how a man and a women get together and make a baby?"

"Oh, no," I said, somehow clueless and confident at the same time.

And this—Magic Johnson's HIV diagnosis—spawned our "birds and the bees" talk. But as he went into the "when a man and a woman love each other very much" spiel, I quickly lost interest and wandered off. I had the attention span of a goldfish, and he had lost his window.

That would soon change, though. Years later, I came running home from school, begging him to explain why all my friends were laughing when the teacher told us to open up our books to page 69. They all had older brothers, so I was always the last one to know what dirty words meant. He explained that I should think of the numbers as people. Like, where their heads would be in respect to one another if they were in that position. As soon as I figured out they weren't standing up, it all made sense.

Everything ended up very HIV positive. Slowly but surely, I learned the truth about the birds and the bees (mostly that birds do not have sex with bees), and Magic Johnson beat a sexually transmitted disease while maintaining the name of a 1980s adult-film star.

VIAGRA AND EARPLUGS

I saw a man at the store purchasing just two things: Viagra and earplugs. That's it. Just Viagra and earplugs. These are the only three scenarios I see happening when he gets home:

Option 1

"Honey, I'm home!" Ned says as he walks in the front door.

"Did you get the goods?" Laura asks.

"Yep!" says Ned, taking his Viagra and handing her the earplugs. "Looks like I'll be able to go all night long, and you won't have to hear my weird sex grunts anymore!"

"Perfect! Let's do this," says Laura, putting the earplugs in and beginning to undress.

Option 2

"Honey, I'm home!" Ned says as he walks in

the front door.

"Did you get the goods?" Laura asks.

"That's enough outta you!" Ned barks, as he puts the earplugs in his ears and pops a Viagra. "Looks like I'll be able to go all night long, and I won't have to hear you yapping the whole time!"

"It's called pillow talk, Ned. And most guys are into that," she says, as she begins to undress.

Option 3

"Honey, I'm home!" Ned says as he walks in the front door.

"Did you get the goods?" Laura asks.

"Yep!" says Ned, popping a Viagra. "Looks like I'll be able to go all night long!"

"But what about our grandchildren?" asks Laura. "The kids left them with us tonight and these walls are paper thin."

"Won't be an issue," says Ned, grabbing the earplugs and walking toward the guest room. "Kids! I've got presents for your ears!"

TROY'S DREAM TRIP TO HAWAII

"Oh my God, it's here," Troy muttered as he pulled into his driveway after a long day at work.

He plopped the box onto his bedroom desk with a thud, took out a knife and began opening it up.

The slick black material shone brightly under the desk lamp's light. Nothing left to do but try it on. He took the helmet out of the box and closed the door behind him. It fit perfectly!

Better yet, it came already charged up. Troy hit the power button on the side and made sure the eyewear was lined up correctly.

A voice came over the helmet's built-in speakers. "Welcome to Ocular Reality," the voice began. "I'm your guide, Octana. Please select your experience."

In Troy's view, a series of thumbnail videos with titles underneath began to appear. There were pages upon pages of experiences to choose from— things like, "Babysitter Wants a Raise," "MILF Needs to Borrow a Cup of Sugar," and the far more blunt, "Get a Blowjob Right Now."

All intriguing options, but Troy wanted a little more than what he could already watch on the Internet for free. He noticed a small bit of text on the bottom right of his periphery that read, "Personalize Your Experience."

"I'd like to personalize my experience, Octana," he said.

"This is your first time. We recommend starting with one of our standard experiences," Octana replied.

"Standard experiences aren't what drove me to spend $1,200 on this thing. I would like to personalize my experience, please."

"As you wish," replied Octana.

The seemingly endless series of thumbnail experiences disappeared, and everything went black.

"Umm, is this thing working?" asked Troy.

Just then, Octana began to speak.

"Troy, your thoughts will be recorded for the next 60 seconds, and will then shape the experience you will soon enjoy," Octana replied. "So I want you to be very mindful of your thoughts during this time."

"Got it."

"I want you to visualize a woman in your life whom you have not been with physically, but yearn for desperately," said Octana.

"Okay."

"Think about every little detail about this woman," she said. "The more details, the more realistic your experience will be."

Being single for the past three years, it was more difficult to narrow it down to *which* woman he yearned for. Predictably, however, his mind went to Alyssa. Over the past year, she had been the one he thought of most consistently during his "alone time." Her curves, her big smile—she didn't even realize how sexy she was, and he loved that.

"Now I'd like you to think of a location you want to be with Alyssa," said Octana.

"Holy shit, you know her name?" he replied.

"Yes, of course. Keep thinking. Twenty seconds left in the Creation Stage."

The helmet was picking up every detail of his thoughts, so he did his best not to wander.

"Think of her voice … her eyes … the way she carries herself … five seconds," she instructed. "Ocular Reality personalization phase complete. I will now exit, and your personalized experience will begin."

The screen faded to black, and then suddenly reemerged to show a gorgeous white sand beach with teal water and gentle waves.

Troy was floored. This wasn't just any beach, it was Poipu, on the south shore of Kauai. It was his favorite beach in the world. The one where he caught his first (and only) wave on a surfboard during a lesson he took on a family trip in high school. This was even more real than he had expected; he could feel the sand squishing between his toes as he walked.

This thing might actually be worth the money, he thought.

He scanned from left to right to get a feel for the helmet's range. It covered his entire periphery vision no matter what angle he chose. A 360-degree view of his favorite beach!

He could see a silhouette of a brunette woman in a bikini making her way toward him. It was Alyssa.

"Could this island be any more beautiful?" she asked.

"I don't understand how it's so empty," he said.

"That's what makes tonight so perfect," she said as she put her arms around him and kissed him hard.

Her lips felt soft and warm, just how he had imagined so many times before. He couldn't even muster up a response further than a smile.

"Make love to me right here on the beach," said Alyssa.

"Are you serious?"

"Yes," she continued. "We're all alone and I want you now."

Troy did not need to be told a second time. They tumbled onto his beach towel as they undressed.

She was on top, as he stared up at her in awe.

"Troy! You feel incredible."

"Oh my God, Alyssa. You feel even more incredible!" he replied.

"What the fuck are you doing?" shouted a voice in the distance.

"I thought the beach was empty," said Troy.

"Who cares?" said Alyssa, still thrusting on top of him."

"Seriously man, what the fuck?" the voice said again, louder this time.

Chris, Troy's roommate, had come home to hear loud banging against the wall in their apartment. Curious, he entered Troy's room after a few unanswered knocks.

There was Troy, completely naked except for a giant black helmet, masturbating furiously as he knocked over furniture and ran into walls.

"You know, most people stop jerking off when they get caught," yelled Chris. "And did you say 'Alyssa?' Are you jerking off to my girlfriend?"

"Damn, Alyssa," said Troy, still going. "I think this Hawaiian dude knows you."

Part 3

Honesty

ADULT BEVERAGES

FIVE-YEAR-OLD: Can I try your drink?

DAD: Sorry son, this is an adult beverage. You can drink these when you're a grown-up like me.

FIVE-YEAR-OLD: Okay. But does it taste good?

DAD: Well, not so much at first. I remember I hated the taste the first few times.

FIVE-YEAR-OLD: Then why did you keep drinking it? I tried orange soda once and it was gross, so I don't drink it anymore.

DAD: Well, a lot of my friends and older people seemed to enjoy it, and I wanted to be like them.

FIVE-YEAR-OLD: My best friend Gavin drinks orange soda, but we're still friends even though I don't like it.

DAD: That's a good point, son. I guess you're more

of a leader than I was at your age. Good for you.

FIVE-YEAR-OLD: Do adult beverages taste good to you now?

DAD: Kinda. With adult beverages, it's less about the taste and more about the feeling you get when you drink it.

FIVE-YEAR-OLD: What does it feel like when you drink it?

DAD: It makes you feel, well, happy. How can I explain this ... you know your favorite blanket?

FIVE-YEAR-OLD: My binky?

DAD: Yeah, exactly.

FIVE-YEAR-OLD: My binky makes me feel safe. Like no monsters can get me if I'm wrapped up in it.

DAD: There you go! That's the perfect way to put it. This drink makes adults feel like they have a nice, warm binky wrapped around them.

FIVE-YEAR-OLD: Wow, so it's like a magic drink that can turn into a binky!

DAD: You're very smart for your age. Have I told you that?

FIVE-YEAR-OLD: Thanks Dad. I can't wait to grow up. I'm going to drink so many adult beverages!

DAD: Well that's the unfortunate part, pal. A few adult beverages makes you feel like you're wrapped in a warm, safe binky, but if you have too many of them things start going very badly, very quickly.

FIVE-YEAR-OLD: How do you know how many you can have before the bad stuff starts?

DAD: If I knew the answer to that question, you wouldn't have to visit me in this trailer park every other weekend.

DEAR OWNER OF THE BRA I JUST FOUND HANGING IN A TREE

We haven't met, but I feel a strange connection to you. Your dirty, white, strapless bra has been dangling off of a branch in a tree on my street for nearly a week, and you have yet to come back and claim it. Is everything okay?

I don't know the backstory behind your loss, so I find myself attempting to fill in the blanks. If I was a betting man, I would put all my money on alcohol playing a heavy factor.

This, Mystery Woman, would lead me to believe that leaving your bra dangling in a tree that night was no accident. I assume you were stumbling home from the bars on Main Street. My friends and I know that route well. Then what? Maybe it was too tight. Too itchy?

I suppose it's understandable, though I thought you might wake up the next morning and want to come back for it. Maybe you just forgot where you left it? Well, I'm here to tell you it was pretty easy to find. It's the one hanging from a tree on Main Street like some kind of tit chandelier.

And let's focus on the biggest mystery of all ... the public bra removal. That couldn't have been easy to do in the middle of a busy street. Did you go full topless? Maybe you took your shirt completely off, then your bra off, threw the bra on the tree, and then put your shirt back on? Or did you do that thing girls can do where they pull their bra out of their shirtsleeve like a sexy magician?

I'll probably never know the answers, but to give myself the best odds, I'm hanging this letter underneath your bra, which is still billowing in the breeze.

W/b, please.

—Robbie

A PLAY-BY-PLAY ACCOUNT OF THE 26 HOURS AND 11 MINUTES MY iPHONE WAS BEING FIXED

9:26 a.m.—Dropped my phone off at the Apple Store.
10:07 a.m.—Already reached into my pocket 47 times.
10:43 a.m.—Just went to the bathroom empty handed. Did you know that pooping doesn't take 30 minutes?
11:29 a.m.—Thought my phone was buzzing in my pocket. It wasn't.
12:53 p.m.—Just had a such a good sandwich! Wish I could take a picture and throw it up on Instagram with the *#foodporn* hashtag.
1:00 p.m.—Siri, what was I supposed to do today?
2:00 p.m.—Spent 20 minutes searching for my phone before remembering I don't have one.
3:00 p.m.—Saw my friend Brian. Made plans to meet at the bar at 7 p.m. No way of updating each

other if something comes up.

4:00 p.m.—Reached into pocket to check what time it was. Eventually remembered I'm wearing a watch.

5:00 p.m.—Wrote, "You know who says muscle weighs more than fat? Fat guys." on a napkin so I wouldn't forget to tweet it when I get my phone back tomorrow.

5:43 p.m.—I'm *positive* my phone just buzzed. Nope.

6:16 p.m.—Could really use my weather app to decide what to wear tonight. Maybe I'll just go outside and feel it out like they did in olden times.

7:00 p.m.—Used watch to ensure punctual arrival at bar. No sign of Brian.

7:02 p.m.—Where the hell are you, Brian? I am so bored. And I don't know what to do with my hands right now.

7:17 p.m.—Two beers deep. Tried to start a conversation with guy next to me, but he's on his phone scrolling through his Facebook feed.

7:23 p.m.—I really think that "muscle vs. fat" tweet has legs. Can't forget about that one.

7:25 p.m.—Finally Brian showed up. He said he texted me to let me know he was gonna be late.

7:45 p.m.—Brian just took a selfie of us and posted it on Instagram and Facebook. Wonder how many likes it'll get.

9:12 p.m.—Beers.

10:52 p.m.—Brian is saying that coffee is a proven

hangover cure. I call bullshit. It's dehydrating. Reached in my pocket to prove him wrong, but can't Google.

12:45 a.m.—Walked home without any music or podcasts. Pure torture.

1:30 a.m.—Bed.

10:18 a.m.—Overslept. No phone to set an alarm.

11:35 a.m.—Made it to the Apple Store without using Google Maps. Way too proud of myself right now.

11:37 a.m.—FINALLY GOT MY PHONE! Checked texts first. Replied to all, and then went to Facebook. Couple pretty funny links, and one video where Mike Tyson fell off of one of those hover boards. Forwarded it to my friend who just bought one of those. Went to Instagram, looks like my friends had fun snowboarding. Cool. Tweeted my fat guy joke. Waiting for some favs. Fuck yeah, just got two in a row.

1:17 p.m.—Dropped my phone in a parking lot. Hadn't gotten a new case yet, so my screen is completely shattered. For the love of God, someone loan me $750, I can't live another twenty six hours like this.

THE ECCENTRIC MILLIONAIRE

MILLIONAIRE: Would you give another man a blowjob for a million dollars?

MAN: Oh, c'mon. Not this stupid game.

MILLIONAIRE: It isn't a game, this is real. Would you give a man a blowjob for one million dollars?

[The Millionaire shows the man the cash in a suitcase.]

MAN: No I wouldn't.

MILLIONAIRE: Really? You'd have a *million* dollars. Think about it. It's kind of a no-brainer. That's enough money to live like a king, and the other part ... it would be over soon enough, and that money could last a lifetime!

MAN: Sure, I'd have a big house and a fancy car, but then at some point I'd have to explain to people how I made a million dollars. Everybody would find out that I'm completely devoid of any sort of moral compass, and lack any sense of personal dignity or self-respect. I mean how incredibly embarrassing, right? No amount of money could make up for that.

MILLIONAIRE: Wow, I never thought of it like that.

MAN: But there's nothing wrong with making a million dollars. Look at you! I need to do what you did. How'd you make your millions, again?

[The Millionaire starts to pack up his suitcase full of cash.]

MILLIONAIRE: Oh you know, little bit of this, little bit of that …

FORTUNE COOKIE WRITER'S BLOCK

"Now listen," James Wong told the four writers in his fortune cookie writing staff. "We've been getting complaints from American customers that they are receiving repeat fortunes in their cookies. We need new fortunes, and we need a lot of them."

"But good fortunes take a long time to write. This is an ancient Chinese tradition!" said Kevin.

"We need quality, yes, but you don't need to be William Shakespeare here. Quantity is our goal." Wong replied. "Now you've been writing all morning, so let's see what do you have for me."

"I've got one," said Nathan. "'Your ambitious nature will help you make a name for yourself.'"

Wong's face lit up. "Boom! An instant classic. This American leaves our restaurant thinking, 'Wow, I'm going to be famous.' Ted, what have you written for us?"

Ted squirmed in his seat. "I wrote a few, but

honestly, I've got a little writer's block."

"C'mon, let's hear them," Wong insisted.

"Umm, it's all just stuff like ... 'Don't worry about money. The best things in life are free.' They just feel like a bunch of obvious clichés to me."

"Same here," said Mitch, another writer. "I wrote 'Big journeys begin with a single step.' I mean, who's going to fall for that crap?"

"Don't sell yourself short, guys, these are pretty good," said Wong. "Americans eat this stuff up, I'm telling you. 'The best things in life are free...' That's not even a fortune, but I guarantee they'll love it. We can crank these out by the boat load!"

"I get it," said Kevin, finally speaking up. "How about, 'There is nothing better than the laughter of a child?'"

"Jesus Christ, Kevin," snapped Wong. "I'll give you a break since you're new. Everyone else, at the count of three, what words do Americans like to add to the end of the fortunes they get? One, two, three ..."

"'In bed!'" Everyone replied in unison, minus Kevin.

"It's pretty much the only reason they like these things," said Wong. "I mean let's be honest. The cookies don't even taste that good."

"I don't understand," said Kevin.

Wong exhaled deeply. "Americans have this little game where they make their fortunes sexual by adding 'in bed' to whatever we write. So basically you just called this customer a pedophile because he's going to read it as him loving the sound of children laughing ... in bed."

"That's the dumbest thing I've ever heard," Kevin said.

"I know it is, but if we want to be successful here in America, we need to keep these customers happy," Wong insisted.

Nathan had an idea. "Okay, then let's do ones like, 'You have something big to offer the world.'"

"... in bed! Genius!" Wong exclaimed. "Now this white guy ... probably named Chad, or Brad, or Thad, will think he has a big penis, and he and all of this friends will laugh and come back to our restaurant many times trying to get another fortune like this."

"But is this worth it?" Kevin interrupted. "James, you're the fourth member of the Wong family to own this restaurant.

"Fortunes used to mean something! These silly little pieces of paper give people hope. We aren't just selling Chinese food. We're selling the idea that you can dare to dream."

James, Nathan, Ted, and Mitch looked at each other.

"'In bed!'" Ted shouted.

"Dare to dream in bed!" said Wong. "That's perfect Kevin, write that one down!"

MILLENNIAL HIGH SCHOOL REUNIONS

EDWARD: Oh, hey Robbie! So good to see you. I can't believe it's been 10 years. I don't think I've seen you since graduation!

ME: I know, time really flies! So much to catch up on. How have you been?

EDWARD: Well I got married last year. We had our wedding in—

ME: Costa Rica, right? Saw the pictures on Facebook.

EDWARD: That's right! It was so beautiful.

ME: Yeah, it sure looked like it.

EDWARD: And we just found out that—

ME: Your wife's pregnant! Twenty-two weeks, if I remember your Instagram caption correctly. I added a week since I think you posted it last Tuesday.

EDWARD: That's ... exactly right. Wow.

ME: Very excited for you.

EDWARD: Thanks! And you're living in San Diego now, right?

ME: Yep, you probably saw—

EDWARD: Your Facebook post. Sure I did. I think I commented "I'm jealous!" with the surfer guy emoji. Because there are a lot of surfers down there, you know?

ME: Oh yeah, I remember that ... I laughed. Great emoji usage, man.

EDWARD: Ha, thanks.

ME: Okay, well I'm gonna go get some punch.

EDWARD: Can we get a selfie first? I need to post a pic of us catching up like this!

CHILDHOOD AMBITIONS

DAUGHTER: Daddy, when I grow up I want to be a princess.

FATHER: You're already a princess, sweetheart. I love you.

SON: Dad, when I grow up I want to be a prince.

FATHER: Oh boy, here we go. Timmy, are you sure you don't want to be a baseball player or fireman?

REVIEWING ONLINE REVIEWERS

Reviewer: Josh G.
Item being reviewed: Twelve-pack of Bounty Paper Towels

"Honestly, these paper towels are just okay. Yeah, they clean up spills, but the quilted texture they advertise didn't really blow me away or anything. It's just like any other paper towel. I'd buy them again, but only because they're pretty cheap."

3 stars.

Reviewer: Me.
Reviewer being reviewed: Josh G.

Josh, if you actually take the time to write a review of paper towels, it better be a passionate one-star or a passionate five-star review. As in, "These paper towels are so durable that they helped me clean up a bloody crime scene, and I haven't been caught yet! Five stars!" Or, "these paper towels are so thin and worthless that they fell apart while picking up my Chihuahua's shit from the floor, and I got Chihuahua shit all over my hands." How much free time do you have, man?

1 star.

Reviewer: Brittany M.
Restaurant being reviewed: Pancho's Mexican Restaurant

"I had a chile relleno and a carnitas taco, both were amazing. Like, SO SO GOOD!!! Maybe the best I've ever had. Before I even ate those, we ordered a pitcher of Pancho's special margaritas, which were spicy but like, in a good way. We also got to see the sunset as we finished our margaritas on the patio! But after the sun went down, it got super cold out on the patio and we didn't bring jackets! We spent the next 20 minutes LITERALLY shivering!"

1 star.

Reviewer: Me.
Reviewer being reviewed: Brittany M.

Shouldn't you be saving that review for Weather.com? Was Pancho supposed to supply jackets with those tacos and margaritas? The most shocking part of your review is that I think you accidentally used the word "literally" correctly.

0.5 stars.
(Half star for admitting you forgot a jacket)

LAST MEAL

GUARD: Holmes! You're aware that your execution by lethal injection is set to take place tomorrow at twenty-one hundred hours, correct?

HOLMES: Yeah. Well aware.

GUARD: Me too ... had it on my calendar for months. Ha ha, I'm kidding, kind of. Now I know you aren't too fond of me, and believe me, the feeling's mutual. But I'm required to take down your last meal request, so let's make this quick.

HOLMES: The last meal I'll ever eat, huh? You always think about stuff like that hypothetically, but you never think it's a choice you'll actually have to make, you know?

GUARD: Oh, did I make it look like I wanted to chat, Holmes? My sincere apologies. Request a steaming pile of shit for all I care.

HOLMES: Take it easy ... this is a big choice! Okay, I guess I'll start with a tofurkey burger with cashew cheese, avocado, shredded carrots, tomato, and pea sprouts.

GUARD: A tofurk-what? Is that a joke?

HOLMES: I'm vegan, Dennis.

GUARD: You're also dead in 24 hours, bud.

HOLMES: I'd like that tofu patty to be the last taste that hits my tongue before I make my way out of this world for good.

GUARD: Tofu? For your last taste? I'm putting you down for a cheeseburger, cause I don't know what the hell you're talking about.

HOLMES: No! I don't eat meat.

GUARD: Why the hell not?

HOLMES: It's unethical! Have you ever seen *Forks over Knives?*

GUARD: Nope.

HOLMES: The movie *Earthlings?*

GUARD: Can't say that I have.

HOLMES: Don't be such a sheep, Dennis. Those cheeseburgers you shove down your fat, stupid face come from cows living in abhorrent conditions.

They're pumped full of hormones so they can have more meat on their defenseless bodies, only to be slaughtered in a pool of their own shit and piss. Not unlike this hellhole I'm stuck in.

GUARD: Did you forget why you're here, Holmes? You slaughtered 27 people and fed their remains to wolves.

HOLMES: A small number compared to the cows and chickens we murder each day. They were meat-eaters, Dennis!

A POET WHO DOESN'T KNOW IT

Poetry is dumb.
What's a haiku, anyway?
Some kind of sushi?

A MINNESOTAN SANDWICH

C-57.

C-motherfucking-57.

I've never had a worse number for a Southwest flight. I usually set a reminder on my phone 24 hours before my flight to check in, but this time it had slipped my mind.

As I made my way onboard, I scanned for an available seat. A flight attendant saw the dumbfounded look on my face and joined my quest to find the one seat in the entire plane that should, according to their system, be open.

"There! Row 3," the flight attendant said.

We had both walked right by the lone empty seat, but no one could really fault us for it. Nestled between two, shall we say "larger ladies," was the last seat on the plane. Hard to see, as there was less than 12 inches of seat cushion visible between them.

They were together, so the flight attendant

asked if they would sit next to each other.

"I like to be by the window," one mumbled.

"I have a bum knee, and I need to be by the aisle so I can stretch it out," said the other.

I resigned myself to the hard truth: I have the worst airplane seat on planet Earth. Phoenix to Minneapolis—the pilot got on the speaker and announced that my prison sentence was to be three-and-a-half hours, gate to gate.

Aisle Lady reluctantly stood up to let me in, and as I sat down, Window Lady greeted me with, "Do you have any snacks? I need to eat something so that I don't get sick."

I've never wished I had snacks in my possession more than I did right then. I rifled through my pockets and bags, desperately searching for peanuts, chips, or anything that could take the image of Window Lady throwing up on my leg out of my mind. I thought she might be bluffing—until she reached into the seat pouch in front of her, grabbed the barf bag from the behind the magazines, and set it right up front. In a "ready position."

As we took off, Aisle Lady began to read an e-mail out loud, over me, to Window Lady. The e-mail was from a relative, who was very happy they had made the journey from Minneapolis for the wedding.

I quickly crammed my ear buds in, turning

on the audiobook for *7 Habits of Highly Effective People*. I needed some positive thinking.

It was clear that these two women were new to airplane travel, most notably when Window Lady began to yell across me over to Aisle Lady, explaining that we were "flying through the clouds right now."

As we hit 10,000 feet, the flight attendants began to make their way down the aisle with the beverage cart. Aisle Lady asked for Diet Coke, and I got water. The flight attended asked Window Lady if she'd like anything to drink.

"Trail mix," she replied.

Unless they had a blender, this wasn't gonna cut it. "To drink, ma'am," the flight attendant replied. "Oh, ginger ale. But I need some trail mix so I don't get sick."

Window Lady would go on to ask the flight attendant for a total of four bags of trail mix, but if it was really helping her not get sick, I'd have offered to run to Costco for her. As she munched away, Aisle Lady began to snore louder than I could even imitate to a friend.

The turbulence didn't help. As a nervous flyer, I found myself lunging for the armrests at every bump. Window Lady gave my knee an "it'll be okay" pat, which was oddly comforting. For the first time, we were on the same team.

The more I thought about it, I realized I

probably had the safest seat on the plane. Being packed so snugly, like an expensive vase marked "fragile," could actually save my life. If we were to go down, Window Lady and Aisle Lady would basically be the bread in a Robbie sandwich. Hell, I'd probably be the only survivor!

Thoughts of being interviewed by the Channel 5 news team swirled around my mind. I could see my name on the bottom left side of the screen with the tagline "Lone Survivor" underneath. A half Hispanic reporter desperately playing up his accent would ask me how I made it.

"Hectór Ródriquez here with the only survivor of Southwest flight 1035. Robbie, how were you able to survive?"

"Well Hector," I'd reply. "I owe it all to Window Lady and Aisle Lady." Hector would look at me, puzzled, so I'd elaborate.

"You see, I had forgotten to check in early on Southwest." (Everyone at home probably gasps.) "And if Window Lady and Aisle Lady weren't on that plane, there would've been no Robbie sandwich. I owe them my life!"

Window Lady was now snoring away, almost in unison with Aisle Lady. I quietly got the flight attendant's attention, asked her for two more bags of trail mix, and laid them on each of their barf bags.

GROUP CHATS ... IN REAL LIFE

Sarah's birthday was in a week, and she wanted to throw a party. It would be far too many people to talk to individually, so she stood up on a table in the middle of the coffee shop and began to shout.

"HEY EVERYONE, I HOPE THIS FINDS YOU WELL. MY BIRTHDAY IS NEXT SATURDAY AND I THOUGHT IT WOULD BE FUN IF WE ALL GOT TOGETHER AND WENT BOWLING! PLEASE RSVP BY FRIDAY SO I KNOW HOW MANY PEOPLE FOR THE RESERVATION. THANKS, CAN'T WAIT TO SEE YOU!"

With that, she sat down and waited for responses.

Jenny was the first to reply. She stood on top of the table across from Sarah, cupped her hands around her mouth, and screamed at the top of her lungs: "COUNT ME IN! WOOOO! BETTER WATCH OUT, MY BOWLING GAME IS ON POINT!"

Everyone in the coffee shop turned and stared.

Worried that the other coffee shop patrons would be angry, Sarah stood on top of the table and screamed, "PLEASE REPLY TO ME PERSONALLY SO IT DOESN'T ANNOY EVERYONE! I REPEAT, DO NOT STAND ON A TABLE AND YELL AT EVERYONE, STARTING NOW!"

Anna walked over to Sarah and whispered in her ear, "I can't make it. I'll be on a business trip."

Sarah whispered back, "No worries, thanks for not shouting to the entire coffee shop. People get really hate that."

"I WILL DESTROY JENNY AT BOWLING!" screamed Tina, before delivering a big wink and flexing her arm.

Sarah felt forced to respond. She got back on top of the table.

"TINA, WHAT DID I JUST SAY ABOUT REPLYING TO ME PERSONALLY? PEOPLE ARE TRYING TO LIVE THEIR OWN LIVES AND WHEN YOU YELL, EXACTLY LIKE I AM DOING RIGHT NOW, IT INTERRUPTS WHAT THEY WERE DOING, ONLY TO HEAR ABOUT A BUNCH OF SHIT THAT DOESN'T CONCERN THEM. AGAIN, EVERYONE, I BEG YOU TO SPEAK TO ME PERSONALLY ABOUT MY BIRTHDAY PARTY. AND EVERYONE ELSE, I'M SORRY FOR ALL OF THIS."

Kelsey, Leanne, and Jordan had had enough. They got up, grabbed their things, and left.

Finally, after about an hour of silence, the coffee shop had appeared to return to its normal atmosphere. Customers were chatting among themselves at normal volumes, sipping on lattes, and people watching.

A few minutes later, Erica barged through the front door. Bumping and pushing her way past the other patrons, she climbed onto the table right in front of the barista and stood up so everyone could see her.

"SORRY GUYS, I WAS AT WORK SO I JUST HEARD ABOUT THIS NOW! BOWLING SOUNDS GREAT, HAPPY BIRTHDAY JESSICA!!!"

PRAYING FOR VICTORY

Kyle paced nervously, trying to gather the courage to knock on the large wooden door in front of him.

"Okay. Here it goes," he assured himself as he gave two soft knocks on the door.

"Yes?" replied a powerful voice inside.

Kyle opened the door and tiptoed inside the office of God Himself.

"Well if it isn't my favorite assistant," said God.

"That's very nice of you to say, sir," Kyle replied.

The office was awe-inspiring. Michelangelo had painted every inch of the ceiling. The energy in the room was palpable.

"I'm sorry to barge in like this, but there's an emergency down on Earth," Kyle said.

"What is it?" asked God.

"My inbox is getting blasted right now, and I just don't know how to play this one. You're familiar with West Plano High School in Texas, right?"

"I'm omniscient, Kyle."

Kyle gave his forehead a "no duh" slap.

"Of course. Well, they have a football game against the Plainview Mustangs, and it's only five minutes until kickoff."

"And?"

"Brian Turner, the quarterback for West Plano is on one knee, looking to the sky and praying to you for victory," Kyle explained.

"That's no emergency. These requests are quite common," said God.

"Very common, your majesty," Kyle agreed. "In fact it is so common, that Travis McDowell, the quarterback for the Mustangs, is on the other sideline with both hands pointing up toward us—toward you—praying for victory as well."

God stood up and began to pace back and forth, scratching his giant white beard as if answer is buried in there somewhere.

"You see how this is tricky? I feel awful. They both go to church, they're good Christian boys. How do we answer both prayers?" asked Kyle. "Do we make the game end in a tie?"

"Kyle," God interrupted. *"How long have you been here?"*

"Six months, sir. Since my car crash," Kyle explained. "I'm sorry, I know I should know the answer to this one, but I don't. I'll get better, but I need your advice just this once."

"Here, I want you to have this," said God,

handing Kyle a golden coin.

"I don't deserve this, I can't even solve a simple prayer dilemma for you," said Kyle, sheepishly.

"*I insist,*" said God.

"Of course, I am so grateful. Thank you! Might I ask, what is the significance of this beautiful coin?"

"*Significance? I just found it in my pocket. Heads, Plainview. Tails, West Plano,*" said God.

"Are you serious?" Kyle asks. "What about the prayers of Travis and Brian?"

"*Or don't flip it. Doesn't matter,*" said God. "*Maybe make them win the game on their own for once.*"

A EULOGY TO MY FINAL ERECTION

Hello, everyone. Most of you know me, but for those who don't, my name is Frederick Williamson. I'd like to start by thanking you all for coming here today to pay your respects. I know if Abner were here with us today he'd be very pleased with the turnout.

I see some of you out there who were very close to Abner. Some of you not so much, but in most cases that seems appropriate. I even see a few I bet he wishes he had known a little better. I'm looking at you, Kelly! And hey, you too, Nikki! You haven't aged a bit.

My relationship with Abner started over 60 years ago. From then on, it was he and I against the world. I'd like to say I was the decision-maker in our dynamic duo, but Abner almost always got his way in the end. He had all the characteristics of a great politician: persuasive, ambitious, and ridiculously confident at times. I think we can all agree on that!

Life isn't the same without you, Abner, that's for sure. I walked right past a gorgeous woman at the pharmacy this morning and didn't even break stride as I went to grab my cholesterol medication. Can you believe that, Abs? I miss you. I miss you so damn much. I'm a shell of a man without you. Remember our secret handshake? Oh boy, here come the waterworks. Can someone pass me a Kleenex? Thanks.

You taught me so much. You taught me to start every day strong. To stand tall and say, "Hello, world!" from the moment I wake up.

If I had known last week would be the last time I'd see you, I would've planned it better. Nikki, I would've begged you to join us. Kelly, your facial expressions lead me to believe you aren't as interested. That's okay.

I know there are several other speakers, so I'll wrap up. Let me end with this:

Abner, you know me better than anyone ever will, and your influence on me over the last six decades was immeasurable. No one will know some of the crazy things we did and the places we hung out at. And don't you worry, I'll keep those memories between you and me ... mainly for legal reasons.

I'd also like you to know that I named you

Abner because it's only one letter away from being "a boner." Get it? Anyway, goodbye old friend … until we meet again.

ACKNOWLEDGMENTS

I'd like to thank my wife. My rock. My voice of reason. My ghost editor. I still can't believe you met a broke stand-up comedian with big, stupid hair when you were 20 years old and said, "yep, that's the guy for me." But I'm forever grateful you did.

And my dad, for reading these stories in their much earlier, poorer drafts. And a lot of stories that didn't make the final cut. You've been my writing hero and mentor since my third-grade book report on *Island of the Blue Dolphins,* and your thoughts and edits drastically improved this book.

And my wonderful, selfless mother, who went to comedy clubs and watched her son tell dirty jokes to strangers so many times. Your unrelenting support gave me the confidence needed to chase my dreams. And I'm sorry for the vulgar, ridiculous things I said while you were in the crowd.

And my supremely talented sister, who showed me what dedication and drive really looks like. You locked yourself in your room with a guitar and a Blink 182 CD at fifteen years old and came out playing Jimi Hendrix and death-metal solos like it was nothing. Never stop playing.

To Yak Manrique and Pari Mathur, two people who I started doing comedy with over a decade ago and were vital to me throughout this project.

The original publishing of this book was made possible through an incredible amount of support through a Kickstarter campaign. And while I owe so much to each and every person who donated, I want to officially recognize the names of several extraordinary donors that helped me reach my goal. Huge thank you to:

Bob and Jeanne
Stephanie, Steven and Ron
Joni and Phil
Emily and Carter
Layne Tally
Jason Rechberg
Shelly Walsh
Lisa Falkson
Troy Pollet

ABOUT THE AUTHOR

Robbie Pickard is a writer and comedian living in Encinitas, California. He toured the country as a stand-up comedian for a long time, but now he writes things like this thing you're holding.

To see his latest work, visit robbiepickard.com.

Printed in Great Britain
by Amazon